AF432104

Fun Writing Prompts to Encourage Creativity

LATE NOVEMBER LEARNING TREE

CREATIVE JOURNALING
Fun Writing Prompts to Encourage Creativity
BY LATE NOVEMBER LEARNING TREE

Published by Late November Literary
Winston Salem, NC 27107

ISBN: 979-8-9988413-2-3

Copyright 2026 by LATE NOVEMBER LEARNING TREE

Cover design by Sweet N' Spicy designs
Interior design by Late November Literary & Sweet N' Spicy designs
Available in print or online.
Visit latenovemberliterary.com

All rights reserved. No part of this publication may be reproduced in any form without written permission of the publisher, except as provided by the U.S. copyright law.

This is a work that includes fictional prompts to support creative writing. Any brand names, places, or trademarks remain the property of their respective owners and are only used for educational purposes.

Library of Congress Cataloging-in-Publication Data:
Late November Learning Tree.
Creative Journaling/ Late November Learning Tree 1st ed.

Printed in the United States of America

A Word of Caution:

Creative writing has been known to unleash imaginations. The results could be incredible stories, dynamic characters, and unlimited fun.

Reader Discretion Advised.

"A professional writer is an amateur who didn't quit."
~Robert Bach

☆ Genre Practice: ☆

Creative Journaling
Genre: Mystery

Jake drags his backpack up his front porch steps annoyed at his teachers for assigning so much homework. Before he opens the door, he stops.

A note with scribbled writing is taped to his front door.
Don't bother looking for them. You'll never find them.

The front door is ajar. He steps inside and the house has been ransacked, and his mother and little brother are nowhere to be found...

What happened next?

____
____
____
____
____
____
____
____
____
____
____
____
____
____
____
____

Officer Smith enters first period English class. "We received a frantic call last night around 11:45 p.m. that six male students, five of which were wearing football jerseys from this very school, were egging the Forest Street neighborhood."

The students glanced guiltily at each other. No one spoke. Finally Eddie, the quarterback, says, "What's the big deal, officer? It's just some eggs."

"It's a big deal because one of the houses that were egged also was broken into the same night and thousands of dollars of jewelry were taken...

What happened next?

____

____

____

____

____

____

____

____

____

____

____

____

____

____

Keep going! This page gives you more room to write.

Old man Snyder has been acting strange. He's always been a little grouchy, but lately, he's been sitting on his front lawn with a shotgun, muttering "They won't take my house! I won't let them!"

Then three black vans approached late one evening. The next morning, Old man Snyder wasn't on his front lawn.

What happened next?

A new family moves into an old house in a quiet neighborhood. Claire, the 15-year-old daughter, starts noticing strange things. Her clothes being moved. Her books disappearing. Doors opening and closing when no one else is home.

Kids at school tell her the old house was abandoned for over 20 years because of a ghost that still haunted the place.

Claire is determined to get to the bottom of it.

What happened next?

Mayor Jackson's dog has disappeared! Soon, other pets start disappearing in the small town of Smithburg. Cats, dogs, birds, even some pet fish.

The 14-year-old twins, Cate and Cal, aren't worried because their large German Shepherd would never let anyone else get close to him.
Until he goes missing too...

What happened next?

Jordan's dad is the local sheriff in Wilson County and is close to retirement.
He can't wait to golf and read newspapers "without interruption."
Then a body is discovered by the river, and it's a person the sheriff
recognizes from his past. Now he and his family are in danger if he doesn't
find out what happened and who did the crime.

Whoever it is, isn't letting go of the past...

What happened next?

It's Your Turn!
Create Your Own Mystery!

Ideas:

Characters:

1.

2.

3.

Conflict:

Setting:

Clues to the Mystery:

1.

2.

3.

Get Writing!

Creative Journaling
Genre: Science Fiction

It's 2035, and each family has been issued a government-prototype robot to "assist in household tasks." Daxton feels uneasy about it, but his single mother says she appreciates the help.

Until one night when Daxton wakes up with the robot standing over him.

What happened next?

George and Ginny's father is about to lead the space exploration of Mars, now that new technology has been developed for them to have regenerative oxygen tanks. The space expedition will take at least 36 months, but their father promises to reach out to them every chance he can.

But one month into the journey, all communication is lost. NASA has no idea what happened, but they cannot find the shuttle or astronauts anywhere.

What happened next?

Aiden hates his new school, and he can't wait each day to run to his grandpa's house and set up the old transistor radio. Eventually, on the evening he and his grandpa have fixed it and put all the pieces in place, a massive thunderstorm hits. Lightning strikes close by, frying the radio's system. Disappointed, Aiden heads to bed. He wakes up to radio static at high volume. With his grandpa still asleep, he decides to investigate without waking him up.
That's when he hears a strange voice speaking in a weird dialect unlike anything he's ever heard. Whatever is being said is being repeated over and over...

What happened next?

Keep going! This page gives you more room to write.

Sally wakes up one morning to find a strange blue bird with yellow wings and black eyes staring directly into her room. She's fascinated by the bird and opens the window to see if it will let her get close. But the bird flies off. The next morning it's there again, looking straight into her window and tapping it with its beak.

She opens the window again, and the bird starts pecking at her arm. Alarmed, she tries to wave it off and shut the window, but the bird is agitated and lets out a large squawk. Suddenly, dozens of the same birds land all around her window.

What happened next?

Landon comes home from school and throws his backpack on his bed. A high-pitched noise startles him. He lifts the blankets and finds a red creature with pointed ears and scaly tail. They both yell, startled.

But the creature doesn't appear hostile, so Landon tries to coax it out from the blankets. It's definitely no animal he's ever observed from earth. What is it? Where did it come from? Landon is determined to find out.

What happened next?

Gentry is Soldier #28973 of Squadron #12 of the Echo Resistance Special Unit. The role of Squadron #12 is simple: travel to the newly discovered planet "Helix" and find the lost soldiers of Squadron #11 and see if there are any survivors.

But there are no communication or visuals once on the planet. So, Gentry and the other young soldiers have no idea what they're stepping into...

What happened next?

It's Your Turn!
Create Your Own Science Fiction!

Ideas:

Characters:
    1.

    2.

    3.

Conflict:

Setting:

Clues to the Story:
    1.

    2.

    3.

Get Writing!

Creative Journaling
Genre: Realistic Fiction

Connor just found out his family is moving cross-country, and he's just about to start his senior year as quarterback at the only school district he's ever went to.

What happened next?

Lilly has to pass math class in order to graduate on time. Her parents hire a tutor, but she has no plans on going. She's too busy working her part-time job and volunteering at the animal shelter.
Her friend showed her a cool app that answers all math questions on her homework and even shows the work. Now all she has to do is not get caught...

What happened next?

The Griffith family is about to go camping for their annual Memorial Day weekend with extended family. Jolie is super excited and can't wait to hang out with her cousins. They've already planned boat rides and early swim contests at the lake.

Then she trips over her suitcase and twists her ankle. Her camping plans are about to be halted...

What happened next?

Jessica decided to try out for the main role in the school's musical of "Annie."
On the day of auditions, she runs into her best friend, Macy, who decided to
try out too. Jessica is upset because Macy kept it from her, especially
knowing how much Jessica wanted the role.
Jessica auditions anyway and tries her best, but then the roles are
assigned...

What happened next?

Sonia is determined to win class president this year. She is tired of "Mr. Popular," Chance Miller, always winning! She makes the coolest posters and even bakes cupcakes for the student body. As the weeks progress, it's becoming clear that she has a good shot at winning.
Until Chance comes over to her and says they need to have a talk...

What happened next?

Henry is stoked about his driver's permit! His dad lets him drive all around their property unsupervised, but he's not to leave the property without supervision.

When Lance calls and begs him to come pick him up for some quality video game time, Henry decides that everything should be fine because Lance is only five miles away. Unfortunately, he wasn't expecting THIS to happen.

What happened next?

Ronnie and Lara have been best friends since his family started attending the same church when they were both five. Now that they're 16, Ronnie wants to ask Lara to the church youth's banquet as a date. When she confides in him that she's hoping to go with the pastor's son, Corey, his hope crashes.

Then Maria asks him if he'd take her instead. He's always thought Maria was nice, but he really wanted to go with Lara.

What happened next?

____
____
____
____
____
____
____
____
____
____
____
____
____
____
____
____
____
____
____

It's Your Turn!
Create Your Own Realistic Fiction!

Ideas:

Characters:
    1.

    2.

    3.

Conflict:

Setting:

Clues to the Story:
    1.

    2.

    3.

Creative Journaling
Genre: Historical Fiction

Victoria Sloan must take the train to a burgeoning new town in California where gold miners have set up camp. Born and raised in Massachusetts, she's never been away from her prosperous New England family. But it's 1850, and it's time she ventures into the world as a 19-year-old schoolteacher.

But she wasn't ready for what she'd walk into...

What happened next?

Augustus may be the Roman emperor's nephew, but he doesn't receive special privileges. If anything, he's forgotten often, only living in the palace because of his parents being killed by the invading northern armies.

When he befriends a servant girl, Lila, he learns about the corruption behind his uncle's empire, but what can he do to stop it? With the help of Lila and other new friends, they may just have a plan...

What happened next?

Henry Billingston may only be 15, but he is determined to follow in his older brother's footsteps and join the Union army. With his excellent shooting and hunting skills, he knows he'll make a fine additional to the Union infantry.

The night he is to pack up and leave, his parents receive word that his older brother was killed in battle. Now he is torn. He is the only son left, and his parents will need someone to help keep the farm.

What happened next?

Sarah Seaver lives in Salem, Massachusetts in 1692. She's been friends with the other girls since her family moved to the area two years earlier. When Abigail, the minister's niece, starts acting strange and falls ill, Sarah goes to visit her. People are whispering, "She's afflicted with something bad. Something not of God." Sarah becomes more worried and hurries to the minister's house. It is there she sees Abigail sneak out of the house, so she follows her to what looks like a secret meeting in the woods with several other girls.

Feeling left out, Sarah doesn't know what to do. Until the girls start pointing fingers at townspeople and calling them witches. Sarah is surprised by this because she knows many of the people they are accusing. Sarah thinks they're lying, and she's wants to expose them. But who will help her? And who will ever listen to her, a 14-year-old new girl from another town? When her own mother becomes one of the accused, Sarah realizes that it is up to her to be brave and find out the truth. Before it's too late.

What happened next?

____

____

____

____

____

____

____

____

____

Keep going! This page gives you more room to write:

It's World War II and Sven wants to marry Helga before the Nazis ever get to Denmark. He asks her to marry him, but she acts surprised and then conflicted. "There's something about me you must know. Something that will change everything."

Helga is an undercover spy, and she's not who she says she is...

What happened next?

____

____

____

____

____

____

____

____

____

____

____

____

____

____

____

____

____

____

____

____

____

It's Your Turn!
Create Your Own Historical Fiction!

Ideas:

Characters:

   1.

   2.

   3.

Conflict:

Setting:

Clues to the Story:

   1.

   2.

   3.

Get Writing!

Creative Journaling
Genre: Fantasy

Rylynn moves into a new house with her parents and little brother. On the first night in the new house, she awakens to a glowing light coming from underneath her bed.

Nervous, she takes a peek and discovers a luminescent door on the floor underneath her bed. Now she's curious, so she gets up and pushes her bed as hard as she can to get a better look. Her hand moves to the doorknob, as she slowly opens the door.

What happened next?

Syske is a part of the Mennog family of dragon slayers. They are fierce and merciless in pursuit of dragons. Without the Mennog family and their long line of descendants, the dragons would have annihilated the human race.

But Syske isn't a fighter; he's a potion maker. He enjoys walking the deep forest of Lin where the creatures are friendly and the trees whisper secrets.

He feels the answers to stopping the fire-breathing dragons can be found with potions that wouldn't kill them but only subdue them.

One night, when he puts a combination of herbs together, it creates a green plume of dust that causes everything around him, including his wolf hound, Toren, in a deep sleep. Could this work on the dragons? Will his family listen?

What happened next?

Keep going! This page gives you more room to write:

Plena must do something or her mother will die of the plague. She's heard of the Zeroth sea monster who lives in the waters of the opal lily, a rare plant with healing powers. Most who try to get the special plant never come back alive. But Plena has no choice. She must try. Her mother is all she has left.

She finds a young man, Barney, who is the son of Pirate Longfellow. She begs him to help her, and he, desperate to get away from the angry fists of his father, readily agrees.

Together, the two young people brave the seas, neither knowing what to expect. Both needing that special plant, the opal lily, but for different reasons. Will Barney betray her for his own gain?

What happened next?

____
____
____
____
____
____
____
____
____
____
____
____
____
____

Keep going! This page gives you more room to write:

____

____

____

____

____

____

____

____

____

____

____

____

____

____

____

____

____

____

____

Britney is excited about spending the night at her best friend's house, Jada. Once there, Jada tells her that she and her mother found this never-been-used before tent at a yard sale. "I thought we could put our sleeping bags in the tent and have our slumber party in there!"

Britney agrees and together, they stock up on snacks and sodas and all the things they want to take with them in the tent that's already assembled on Jada's back porch. "It's a perfect night," Britney says, then steps into the tent with Jada.

Suddenly, the earth shakes beneath their feet. They hurriedly exit the tent, but they are no longer on Jada's back porch. They are now standing in a thick forest with large insects. They hear a roar not far from them. They turn to each other and scream!

What happened next?

____

____

____

____

____

____

____

____

____

____

____

Keep going! This page gives you more room to write:

Jared travels to Madagascar with his family for a mission's trip. He is irritated because he's missing the entire homecoming week including the parade, the football game, and the dance.

One day while handing out bottles of water to an impoverished area of town, an older man approaches him with a cup of blue liquid. "Drink this," he says, "And your greatest desire will come true."

Jared scoffs and says, "Thanks, but I'm not falling for that."
The old man shrugs. "Okay, but I know how badly you want to go home. One drink and that can be a reality..."

The old man walks away, leaving Jared staring into the cup of blue liquid. He smells it, and it smells sweet like fruit. "Maybe I should try it," he says to himself. "What would it hurt?"

What happened next?

Keep going! This page gives you more room to write:

It's Your Turn!
Create Your Own Fantasy!

Ideas:

Characters:

1.

2.

3.

Conflict:

Setting:

Clues to the Fantasy:

1.

2.

3.

Get Writing!

Creative Journaling Genre: Fairytale Reimagining

Elizabeth is an orphan and lives in a kingdom far away with her mean uncle and aunt. They treat her like a servant and barely provide for her, making her live in the barn with the farm animals.

One day, she finds a lost horse with the kingdom's emblems upon its chest. She takes it to the palace, hoping for some coins so that she can afford to eat a proper meal when she comes face-to-face with the prince. It was his horse that he fell off during a hunt.

What happened next?

Leona is forced to stay in a tower upon the formidable Cliff of Doom. Her distant father, the king, keeps her there because that is how he earns gold and jewels from young suitors paying for a chance to scale the cliff and retrieve her. Not one has ever made it to her.

When Logan, an on-the-run petty thief, sees the cliff and high tower, he hopes that it will keep him away from those who pursue him, not knowing who is inside. With his unmatched strength and skill, he climbs the cliff.

What happened next?

Prince Mowi must find the stone of sage in order to take his place as heir to the Persian throne of his father. This daunting task will have him traveling through desert and jungle, fighting beast and foe, with only his sword and an ancient compass to guide him.

When he comes across Nalia, daughter of a traveling gypsy, he becomes distracted, not realizing that he is a valuable commodity that could fetch her and her father a hefty sum. But she has fallen for him too...

What happened next?

Pick any fairytale that you have read (or a fairytale adaption in movie form) and change the ending!

- Choose a common fairytale where you know most of the traditional story.
- Rewrite it with a twist! How would you change the ending to make it more powerful? Or humorous? Or shocking?

Change the story and ending here:

It's Your Turn!
Create Your Own Fairytale!

Ideas:

Characters:

    1.

    2.

    3.

Conflict:

Setting:

Clues to the Fairytale:

    1.

    2.

    3.

Get Writing!

Creative Journaling Genre: Thriller & Suspense

Johnny is running late for work. He jumps into his car after basketball practice and sighs. He only has five minutes before he's late, and his job is fifteen minutes away.

As he speeds down Main Street, the light turns red. He slams on his brakes, frustrated. Just then, his back door opens, and a guy with a gray hoodie pulled over half his face, points a gun at him. "Do as I say, and you won't get hurt..."

What happened next?

____
____
____
____
____
____
____
____
____
____
____
____
____
____
____
____
____
____

Rachel doesn't like her best friend's new boyfriend. He acts possessive and needy. Soon her best friend starts to pull away from Rachel, saying that her boyfriend needs more time with her. Rachel is hurt, but she tries to give her best friend space.

Then one day, her best friend shows up at Rachel's house with bruises and a black eye. She says she's scared because her boyfriend promises that there will be consequences if she goes to the police.

The two of them try to decide what to do when a car screeches right outside Rachel's house. Neither of her parents are home. Rachel tries to call them and leave a message, but the pounding at the door interrupts her.

What happened next?

Keep going! This page gives you more room to write:

Janey loves babysitting the Murphy's kids. The kids are three and six and so cute! One night, the Murphys are gone later than anticipated. She was expecting them before midnight, and it's past 2 a.m. Janey has church in the morning and doesn't sleep well on their couch. She's tried to call and text, but neither one of them are responding. She checks on the children, and they are sleeping fine.

That's when she hears a windowpane breaking by their front door.

What happened next?

Zeke and Joshua meet a new guy at work, named Blane. He's funny and likable, and soon, the three are hanging out all the time. One night, the three of them decide to head to Coney Island and hang out at the rides. When all three admit they're broke, Blane tells them not to worry. Then he pulls into a small gas station and tells them to wait in the car. "No matter what. Don't come inside." Zeke feels uncomfortable and tells Blane not to do anything stupid, but he's already left the car.

After a few minutes, Zeke and Joshua are freaking out because they can see in the window that Blane is yelling at the cashier. Suddenly, gun shots ring out, and Blane comes running outside. As he starts the car and peels away, he starts to sob. "It wasn't me!" he's crying. "I swear, it wasn't me!"

Zeke and Joshua turn to each, neither knowing what to believe. They are terrified that something bad is going to happen.

What happened next?

Keep going! This page gives you more room to write:

Caison walks around the history museum, ready to leave. But the field trip isn't over yet. Feeling bored, he leaves the group and starts exploring the halls. Not realizing how far he's wandered, he turns down a darkened hallway with only small offices on either side. "I better turn around," he thinks to himself.

Just then, he hears voices. They begin to shout at each other. There's a loud pounding, a scream, and then a man in a tweed jacket comes barreling out of one of the offices, holding a large rock.

Even though the hallway is dim, Caison thinks he sees red on the rock. And now that man is running toward him.

What happened next?

Keep going! This page gives you more room to write:

It's Your Turn!
Create Your Own Suspenseful Story/Thriller!

Ideas:

Characters:

   1.

   2.

   3.

Conflict:

Setting:

Clues to the Story:

   1.

   2.

   3.

Get Writing!

Creative Journaling Genre: Action & Adventure

Drake closes the gate behind the last cow. The wind has picked up, and the rain has started pelting down. He adjusts his hat and looks for his dad. "He shouldn't be out there in this," he thinks to himself. He calls him on the cell phone, but his dad doesn't answer. Typical. When Drake left him, he was still fixing the tractor's belt.

Just then the tornado siren sounds. Drake's mom rings the bell from the back porch. "Get to the cellar!" she bellows for anyone within the sound of her voice. Sighing, Drake jumps onto the four-wheeler. He needs to get his dad, or he'll never hear the end of it from mom. Drake zooms across the fields, still hearing his mother caterwauling behind him. The sirens have yet to let up, so Drake urges the four-wheeler to go even faster.

Almost to his father, he sees the spiral of a tornado in the distance. He's got minutes. "Come on, Dad!" he yells, motioning for his dad to stop tinkering with the tractor. Thankfully, his dad listens. He shuts his tool box and carries it over to Drake who is still eyeing the tornado that's inching closer.

what happened next?

____

____

____

____

____

____

____

Katrina hugs her mom and dad goodbye before heading into the airport. She is off to visit her grandparents in Boston. This isn't the first time she's flown solo, so she follows the procedures she knows to do. When she's finally seated in the airplane waiting to take off, she pops her headphones on, and closing her eyes, she leans back and starts listening to music.

She must have dozed because she suddenly awakens to intense shaking. This is the most turbulence she's ever felt. When the masks drop and the pilot announces that everyone needs their oxygen masks on and to brace for an unexpected landing, she starts to panic. She glances outside the window to see they're flying over the Appalachian Mountains.

With her mask in place, she holds the seat tightly and says a prayer. The turbulence is so intense, and the descent is so rapid, that Katrina wonders if she'll make it out alive.

What happened next?

____

____

____

____

____

____

____

____

____

____

Keep going! This page gives you more room to write:

Bobby Bolling is the youngest race car driver in the Xfinity Series of races, and many say he has the skill of making it to NASCAR one day.
As he preps for the race, he feels excitement, ready to win big.

When Sal Matley approaches with a group of other drivers to chat with Bobby, it is clear that they are not there on friendly terms. "Watch your back," Sal says as he walks away. "The only one winning today is me." Bobby rolls his eyes and continues to get ready.

"Start your engines!" is called on loudspeakers. Bobby is in position, and he's revving his engine, waiting for the flag to signal to start. Bobby roars past the others, and he and several others race neck and neck around the tracks. One lap. Two laps. It's close, and Bobby is fully concentrating.

Suddenly a rattle begins, then a tire is loose, and Bobby's car flips over and over. It happens so fast, Bobby doesn't even register what is happening until he spells gasoline. He's got seconds, but his seatbelt is stuck.

What happened next?

____
____
____
____
____
____
____
____

Keep going! This page gives you more room to write:

Rhonda loves going camping with her dad. The two of them fish and eat off the land. One morning, he tells her that he's going fishing, but Rhonda wants to sleep a little longer. "It's okay," her dad says. "Sleep in. I'll be back in an hour or so." That's all the invitation Rhonda needs! She falls right back to sleep until she is woken up by some noise from outside her tent. She listens then goes completely still. A large animal is outside! It's sniffing at things and knocking them over.

She slowly unzips the tent and sees a large brown bear and two of her cubs destroying their campsite.

What happened next?

Jonathan and Andrew have been boy scouts and best friends since they were eight years old. Their favorite part of the year is the annual camping trip with their troop. Now that they are fifteen, they will help lead others and hopefully earn another patch.

Their troop hikes for miles through Blue Ridge mountains of North Carolina. They won't stop until they reach camp, which isn't for a while. Little Timmy has complained and had slowed down the rest of the group. He's only twelve, and he is much smaller than the other boys. The troop leader asks Jonathan and Andrew to keep an eye on Timmy. But he becomes so far behind that all three of the boys have lost sight of everyone else.

Just then, the sky darkens, and the rain begins to pour...

What happened next?

Keep going! This page gives you more room to write:

It's Your Turn!
Create Your Own Action & Adventure!

Ideas:

Characters:

    1.

    2.

    3.

Conflict:

Setting:

Clues to the Story:

    1.

    2.

    3.

Get Writing!

Creative Journaling
Genre: Humor

Jackson and his older brother, Maxx, are always fighting. Maxx is an important high school basketball player who's also a top scholar. Jackson is a 9th grader who hates sports and most classes and only wants to build his own computer for major game playing.

When suddenly an argument goes haywire, they feel a shock between them. They discover they have switched bodies! Oh no! Maxx has a major game, and Jackson just entered the science fair with his newly assembled computer.

What humorous event happened next?

Dylan is tired of the substitute teacher, Mr. Lomes, who is an old, mean man who spits while he yells at students. Dylan and his friends decide to play the ultimate prank on Mr. Lomes to get him out of their classroom for good.
But the prank doesn't go as planned...

What humorous event happened next?

Kayley finds a lost dog on her way home from school. He follows her even when she stops and orders the dog to go away. But he doesn't listen. Now at the house, the dog stops at the door beside her. "Go away!" she yells. "No," the dog says clearly. "I'm thirsty and hungry."
Kayley nearly falls over in shock. "How are you talking to me?"

What humorous event happened next?

Robby wakes up one morning and goes to leave for school. His mom asks him a question, but when he responds, he's talking in a completely different language! He stops and looks at his mom strangely. "What's going on?" she asks. "I didn't know you could speak French."

French? Robby answers that he doesn't know any French, but the language that comes out is definitely not English!

What humorous event happened next?

Laney follows her father into a pawn shop. She's already bored, and she knows her dad will take forever trying to trade his baseball cards for top dollar.

"Psst... Over here." Laney turns to see an older woman on the other side of the counter. "This is for you." It's a small writing device that looks like it's part pen but part pencil. "No, thank you." Laney goes to walk away, but the old lady stops her and puts the pen in her hand. "Oh no. IT chose you. Good luck."

What humorous event happened next?

It's Your Turn!
Create Your Own Humorous Story!

Ideas:

Characters:

    1.

    2.

    3.

Conflict:

Setting:

Clues to the Story:

    1.

    2.

    3.

Creative Journaling Story Time!

What Genre? (Choose all that interest you. Will you merge genres together?)

Working Title: (You can change this; Come up with a couple ideas.)

1.

2.

3.

Cast of Characters: (Who will be the protagonist? The antagonist? The comic relief? The best friend? The love interest?)

1.

2.

3.

4.

5.

Setting: (Will it be on earth? On another planet? In another world?)

Important Plot Points: (Don't hold back! What are some events or situations that you want to happen in the story?)

-
-
-
-
-
-
-
-

The Major Conflict: (This conflict is PIVOTAL to the story; describe it.)

Beginning:

Middle:

118

Ending:

Thank you for supporting

Late November Learning Tree!

Consider our other educational workbooks:

Journaling for Kids

Journaling Is Writing Too!

Journaling through Scripture

Paragraph Practice

Essay Writing

Poetry Practice

Sight Words 1 & 2

...and more!

Visit us at www.latenovemberliterary.com

www.ingramcontent.com/pod-product-compliance
Lightning Source LLC
Chambersburg PA
CBHW081220130726
47997CB00009B/2735